KV-372-486

FINDING THE CURVE

FINDING THE CURVE

May Ivimy

with Love to
Dorothy Francis,
from
may Badman
of Ivimy 24/2/0??

Shoestring Press

All rights reserved. No part of this work covered by the copyright
hereon may be reproduced or used in any form by any means –
graphic, electronic, or mechanical, including copying, recording, taping,
or information storage and retrieval systems – without written
permission of the publisher.

Typeset and Printed by Parker and Collinson Ltd.
Nottingham NG7 3FH
(0115) 942 0140

Published by Shoestring Press
19 Devonshire Avenue, Beeston, Nottingham NG9 1BS
Telephone: (0115) 925 1827
www.shoesstringpress.co.uk

First Published 2007
©Copyright: May Ivimy

ISBN: 978-1-904886-48-8

For my husband,
Ray Badman

Contents

LIGHT FINGERS

You came in daylight
At the shopping hour
Slid through the hedge
Limbed lightly up to the balcony
And found the only door we'd left unlocked.

Quick in the bedroom, you touched everything
Yet left everything untouched
Save a watch which clung to your thumb.

Downstairs you bolted our door,
Our exit and our entrance
And opened your means of escape.
From room to room you stepped
High heeled like Pan, flinging
All inner doors wide
And took a clock.

Why did you come?
So little suited you.
A fast worker,
But you took your time.
We blundered in, you flew
Safe and away
Between the silence
Along the dumb lane.

And yet
You have never left.
We share our house
With you.

URBAN CHILDHOOD

As a child I ran in a country of bricks,
Through a land of high buildings. Tall
Trams curved and tottered over
Cobbled hills, the sun ran
From rooftop to rooftop flicking
Chimney shadows.

It all seemed hostile. People
Stared and pushed. My turn
Never came, my question, hardly asked,
Was ignored. Even the nosy dogs
Seemed to be saying 'Shall we
Bite you, little girl, who
Doesn't belong
In these streets?'

And the great dray horses chose their moments
To clash and spark their giant hooves
When I was alongside, or shocked me
With their sudden steaming water
Flooding the gutter. Fear pinned me
In the narrow streets, between
Sweating horse-flanks, whipping draymen,
Ironclad wheels, and walls of stone.

Yet there were afternoons when the sun stood still
And the pavements were empty.
A solitary sparrow pecking
On flattened dung. A butterfly sunning
On a clipped privet.
I would wander then, in the tree-lined streets,
Invisible in my paradise of loneliness,
No evidence of my soul,
Just my shadow
And a silent eddy of dust.

TRAIN WHISTLE

Remember the room, north facing, cold, and laced
With fog which outside rotted the bricks,
The gutters, the very air.
Remember the iron bed, its cotton quilt
Stiff as a tombstone, still
Hoarding what light there was
In its miserly white.

Remember the whistle, teasing a child's ears
Going on and on and on. What is it?
An engine somewhere, nothing. Go to sleep.
Why does it whistle all the time? Don't ask me.
It is stuck in the fog, or broken down.
It doesn't concern you. Go to sleep.

Cold covers, hard pillow, and in the creeping dark
The far-off whistle of an engine in distress.
Perhaps it can't see the way, perhaps
The lines have gone, perhaps the driver
Has got his finger stuck, perhaps
The engine has fallen over and can't get up.
Why don't they go and help it?

The house bricks melt, and all the miles between
The darkling bed and the bleating engine
Are a tangled mess of torn and twisted metal. The bed
Lurches to iron feet, moves out and over the waste.
I'm coming, shrills the child, Wait - I'm coming.

GREASEPAINT

Down the road was the Empire.
He'd done the electrics there,
Painted some of the scenery.
He had his own make-up box,
Made up some evenings to be ready for a stand-in.

At home was his wife.
She hated the stage.
False, she said, all lies,
Fearing the cooked-up emotions
Erupting under the lights.

At home too were the round faces
Of two mannikins
He could play with.

He pushed the chairs about,
Inventing a rushing, rocky stream,
Stood the girl on the bank of it
Cradling a doll in her arms.
The make-up round her mouth was bitter.
The skirt got in the way of her feet.

He put the boy on a chair
On the opposite bank.

He told the girl to weep and cry
How she would drown herself and her child

And he told the boy to cry out
'Wait, I will save you!'
And to jump into the river.

The child hesitated,
His moustache slipping,
But at the roar of command repeated
He jumped into the swirling water,
Fell on the boulders, and weeping

Stumbled across the room to his mother,
Buried his face in her skirts.

The girl thought about the plot.
She blamed the baby.

THE OTHER HALF OF THE BED

The other half of the bed is empty,
Cool where warmth once radiated
From his hard long limbs. I use it now
As a place to leave my books, and tomorrow
As I drink my morning tea I shall
Spread our letters there, his and mine.

The time between, when I pull the light
And the dark drops down and kills today,
When now is not today, and not tomorrow,
Is when my feet will stray
Searching for the warmth that is not there,
When I shall have no signal when to turn,
No heavy arm to belt me down
And sentence me to sleep. Upon my lids

He will float in his iron bed, in his bright far ward,
Lit up there, and with glass between us.

DEATH WAS IN NO CORNER

Death was in no corner
That night.
He had her. He wore
His grin of possession, allowed her
The wave of one weak hand
Before going.

Death had a ball
That night.
He'd taken her slowly
Over weeks. What he left
We were glad to bury.

Grief
Was like knives. We stood
Split to our roots, half
Unearthed round the cold
Pit of her unbeing.

DEAD END

I met her at Christmas.
Over her shoulder the shade of her problem
Wore her own diffident smile.

She was cool and thin.
Her hand allowed
The briefest clasp.

Her dead-end loves had been
Her mother, their house, their cats.
One by one they had gone.

She remained, a vessel drained,
A servant
With none to serve
Save one frail animal
She knew was dying.

That is the story, set up by life;
Or perhaps a deliberate course, how can you tell?
We all enter the maze. Some
Are so clever at choosing
All the dead ends.

But she wrote the final chapter -
The slender, empty vase of her
Retained a secret dreg, a choice
She yet could drain.

In the New Year
She tidied her hair, her person,
And that cold shell, her room.

She wrote neat notes.
She swallowed a hundred aspirins
As you or I
Might have boarded a bus
Headed for a distant town.

One item she misjudged, or two.
The dying cat hung on
For six sad weeks grieving;
And for those who nursed it,
And who buried them both,
There was indeed, what might have shaken her,
A very tender pain.

LEAVING

It was as if in the middle of conversation
That she died, my mother.
She had ordered the sweep and when he came
There was no-one to cope with him,
And after the funeral of her brother that day
There was no-one to make tea and put out cakes
For the returning mourners.

She had never liked funerals.
Even for her brother she would have stayed back
To have the kettle hot and the table laid.

Her luggage was all packed for her visit to us,
Which had been put back for the funeral,
In the end her own, and forever,
Which was why it all seemed so awful
That she should go, like that, leaving everything.
It was not like her at all.

RODMELL
(Virginia Woolf's Bedroom)

They have set up her room as he had it
With things that were hers or could have been hers
The narrow white bed beneath the window
Her bed or the ghost of her bed
Where once she lay, while the birds talked in Greek.

She was not mad then
But sane, and longing for comfort, listening, lying there
Her long feet aching for freedom to run on grass
Which lapped at the very door of her room,
Watching the low trees by the window
Where the birds talked, as birds do,
In their own tongue, which
Since she anyhow understood,
May well have been Greek.

THE VISITOR

I said to him 'Why
Have you come so late?'
        He lifted his wings
Slightly, his way
Of shrugging his shoulders.
        His beak
Of pure gold opened a little
And his tongue gave a cheeky
        Amethyst loll.

'Take a chair' I said, 'if you'd like to.
        The cakes I made
Are still fresh, and the elixir
        Is in the refrigerator.'

On ivory talons he crossed the grass
        To the chairs
And he took his perch
        On the back of one,
Arranging his gorgeous tail and smoothing a feather
On his gleaming breast. I went
        To fetch drinks and in each
I popped a diamond. The biscuits
        Were flakes of gold, they
Had cost me the earth.
        He drank, bending his head,
Clattering the jewels in his crest.
        I sat, passing him food
And we conversed
        Until dusk. A moon
Rose from the trees. He leapt
        Silently from his chair

And brushing my hand lightly
        With one wing tip, he said
'I must go. It's been so nice. I'm sorry
        I was late.'

I watched him go. His great wings
        Lifted him over the hedge
And for a moment I saw his
        Glittering outline
      Against the moon.

THE WOMAN WHO RODE AWAY

Life wanted to marry me
And lately did,
But I'm no wife,
It isn't in me.
Amanuensis, helpmeet,
Neither's my role.
While others sweep, I sleep,
While others sleep
I must work my dream.

So saying, the woman
Dragged her bicycle from the shed
And rode away.

Bicycle clips
Were long afterwards discovered
In the Mexican desert,
And a pump
By the Pyramids.

Everest has collared
The front wheel
And the rest of the machine
Can be seen
In a glacial chasm.

She pedals on
Amongst the stars,
Her children
Forever calling.

I SEE THINGS IN A CERTAIN WAY

I see things in a certain way,
I listen for the voices.
I get on with things
And am not exalted, manufacturing
Out of my own head
Nothing.

Quiet in my home
I hear the sirens of far-off fires,
Reflect sunset as a mirror.
The whole earth's cry
Is mine.

In my sleep I know
When the moon bites the curtains
And the streets run with fire
And the clattering hooves
Of maddened horses.

And I rest, singing
'Who will draw us to heaven?
A cat,
A camel and a duck,
As it was said.'

CAT

Hold her claws in your cupped hand loosely,
Feel them quiver in a rage of love.
Move the dense fur over her small skull,
Finger her muzzle closed
Small, tight as a winter bud.
When it opens see the orchid cavity,
The white metal fangs.

If you were dead she might wonder
Why you lay so still.
She would sit on your face and assume
You were the meat you always give her.

THE ENEMY DARK

Out here in the lane
Emeralds in pairs flash out
Laserbeaming the enemy dark.
They are not the eyes of Tiger,
Nor Wee Georgie, grown big now,
Long limbed and rich in rufus fur.
At home their eyes are agate, amber,
A soft black, an innocent dreamy yellow.

Out here in the lane
These green disembodied brilliants
Manifest the universal cat soul,
And deep behind my nightblindness
Another animal stiffens
And reaches slowly back
For a handsized rock.

CATTLE

The cattle have noticed us.
Two of them stand and stare
At us as we at them.
We stand on the broad road and they
Below smooth hills in a passion of green.

The rest meander on, perhaps to the milking.
These two, across a furlong and a low hedge
Stare. Has the milking changed?
Is the milking not up here,
But over there? They are trapped.
They cannot move out of their idea.

They cannot leave the considering,
They cannot answer their own question.
We stare. They stare.
And the last of the others has left them,
All but these two have hastened up the hill.

Then we laugh, and release them; far off as they are
We see their bewildered eyes,
Their twitching muzzles, dripping
A green stem; we let them go.

We begin desultorily to walk,
Continuing along the road,
And they turn their bony heads
And plunge gracelessly up the slope
After the others' swaying buttocks, their slashing tails.

MARCUS

Outside our door, morning is perfect,
A blue and white affair,
The sun crashing silently through a high mist,
Clouds linen-cased pillows, bundled in sleep,
Field grass gleaming from yesterday's rain.

The two donkeys are posed, quiet,
On their lily white legs,
And Marcus, the centre-piece
Sleeps on the field, a sculpted bronze,
His haunch spot-lit in the low-swept light.

From down in the empty lane, where I stand,
I can see his head, in the daisies,
And his ear, a sharp dark point.
At my low whistle
It flicks, just the once
As his sleep, like a blanket
Takes him back.

HAWTHORN

When I was young they told me
My plant brought evil with it under a roof
And so I believed my luck was bad, and kept aloof,
A witch on the outskirts, one who would never settle,
Nor marry nor breed, a solitary kettle
On a secret hearth, and a cot where none would hold me.

EATING HONEY

Gentle, amber stream,
Smelling of hive sweat,
Something greater than sweet;
An invisible strength
Buzzes like bees in my blood.
I become
The Queen, giving and giving and giving
From my royal abundance.

MAN AT WORK

He works on, keeping his daylight eyes
Far into the dark; he seems oblivious
Of the threatening beauty of the new year sky
Which behind him makes a cliff-edge
Of the garden down which the daytime runs.

Under his hands
The simple, gripping vision holds,
Of wood waiting on wood, of nails
Biting precisely, hammer-helped
Into their fated places, and the construction
Grows like a cloud, black and real,
As even now
Long planks of cirrus nail themselves
Rose flushed along the violet west.

AUNTS

Aunts are cleaner now.
Aunts shower every day, and their corsetry
Such as it is, spins in suds after a day's wearing.
Aunts are teachers, or social workers, they are computer buffs.
They ski, sing madrigals, take a bus across India.
Fur stoles, camphor and whalebone have been dead
For a hundred years.

Yet aunts are aunts. Not quite mothers.
Politer, and they give you treats, and let you stay up late.
They give you lots,
But you owe them nothing.

MEN

A man's face
Is not exactly a shop window,
Treasures not on show
Nor or sale,
More an edifice with blinded
Windows, a cliff
Prolific of crevices
Where sea-birds nest,
Where they nurture
Days when they saved the nation,
Fires they fought through,
Hurts, woundings, deaths.

So we look, and warm to them,
Want to serve them
Baked beans on toast,
Take off their uniforms,
Leave their medals.

SHADOWS

Until now nothing swept across my field
But the shadow of a lark,
The chalk line of a high plane,
Hang-glider ambling in air,
Sunday balloon painted on the sky
Its match-flame playing a morse signal,
Its gasping roar a thirsty dragon.

Now, the ghost of a laden cloud;
Sandbags, sirens, the silent flame,
Trees and houses crumbling like shadows
When the light sweeps forward.

AT THE TIME OF THE MOCK INVASION

I remember the heat of that day,
And the wavering air above the gravel,
And the bluish tinge of the hedgerows
Around ripe cornfields.

I remember the weight of the dallying child within me,
And the long rough path down which
My son had run, careless and happy,
To meet the soldiers.

I remember the lane at the bottom, full of armour,
The tanks, massive, palaeolithic, moving thunderously
In the planned exercise towards
The defeated village.

I remember that the sight of the slow, unstoppable procession
Shoved against my mind,
That I felt a fool, with my big belly and lank hair,
Shapeless dress, legs bare to the weather,
In this gutter of my femininity before that achieved peak
Of the ordered male. The little heads
Of the men stuck out from the high turrets
And shot me grins and shouts as I saw
High-riding on one of the tanks, my son.

'Leave him be, missis!' they hollered, when I called him.
'Let the little bugger have his fun!'

THE GREAT GREEN HILL

The great green hill held her high and away from me,
The steep years that divided us, her tallness,
Her woman's skirt and piled hair, dark above her white blouse,
So much beyond me up there, the sky and a large tree behind her.

The way up was almost too much for me, yet it could not be,
                         and I had to climb
Without stopping, to her side. It was a command I had laid
                         upon myself
And I could do no other than obey. If I scrambled, finally,
                         to the top,
And flung myself down upon her spread out skirt, saying
                         nothing -
If she laid her hand lightly on my head as I lay
Smothering my gasping breaths, hiding my face in triumphant
                         shame
(Knowing I had given far too much to the fantasy) -

I do not remember, I do not remember. All I recall
Is the steep green hideous mound, and my slow, impossible
Conquering of it.

INNOCENT LIGHTS

I fell in love with you then,
But there was a war on.
I had heard and read about you
But had not seen
The glittering dew, the grass lights,
Had not rooted brave fingers
Into wet grass, at dusk
Feeling for the small grey body
With a cool green torch on its tail.

Poems were words about words,
Words about dreams. Once we met
It was the real thing. I sat back to a haystack;
Scented and rough, it was as solid as a house.
It was my Mother, and the sun
In his amber evening warmth was
God the Father. There, set out before me,
Was the play dance of brothers and sisters,
Field rats, happy, warm and full,
Leaping in the joy of living.

Of course I fell in love. Every tree
Was a friend, grasshoppers companioned,
Grass itself, laid out everywhere
Was love. But the war was on.

That hesitated, hung up there,
Over there, then, smash.
It was on us. In all that scorching,
Crashing, breaking, love
Like grass, went underground.

And when the war died,
In the years of unease that followed,
Slowly grass and love grew back.

Now, again, I am in love.
But it isn't quite the same.

Some of the jewels you gave me are here
But I wait, and hope
For the glow worms, their innocent lights.

BOXES

First, I had a shoe box.
In it I kept a stone
And called it my museum.

Next I had a room.
In it I kept a baby
And called it home.

Some day I'll have a wooden box
Below the ground.

I shan't keep a baby in it,
Nor yet a stone.

I'll be a relic in it
And call it my museum.

PIGGY BANK

I bought it at a fete
For twenty pence,
A tired-of toy.

It has a doll face, parody
Of human, not pig.
In full light it is cheaply pretty,
Pastel and floral.

Now by some accident it stands
Back to the light of wind and rain,
Full face to me. I see

The glossy pot sides,
The dark slit,
And the face in shadow,

Blue eyes grown black,
The simper, stern. It has
Still the penny only that rattled
Inside it when I bought it.

I spend myself as I go
And there's never anything left
To save. There are too many
Rainy days. I shall be empty
At the end.

BAD WEATHER IN AN OLD GARDEN

The sky is dull and oozing a lazy rain,
The creeper is reaching with new hands across the wall,
The oak leans south away from the northern blast
And blooms beneath scramble and fall to their knees,
Greedy, thirsty for the sun's mean light.

All of the garden is a place
Of small triumphs, gross defeats.
Rose heads shine, tall women in a crowd,
And as you pass the beds it is the nettle
That presses a sting into your hand,
A beggar giving alms.

BALANCE

When I stop to consider
What Earth is, and that I am on it
Balanced on two feet on a rough ball
Balanced in a constant flight round the sun,
The sun a mass of fire and flame, balanced
On its own flight looping the galaxy
Which circles . . . what? (the astronomers see
A patch, a smear, of something dark)
We don't know yet -

I feel as I did my first time riding a bicycle,
When my father let go my shoulder
And those wheels spun, with me balanced
On how much of two tyres where they touched the road
Bowling me along at a new speed.

REPETITIONS AND DEVIATIONS

Each day I feed the cats and birds
And grieve in passing
That I have not hoovered the house for ages
And have bought too many books and
Too many plants in pots and too many clothes,
And haven't been to church nor prayed exactly
But I do think, yes, I think and wonder
And ponder about all these wars
And starvations and people in Africa and London
With no money and nowhere to live, and
I think it is not good literature to have all those 'and's
And no conclusion, and how can there be
When the great question behind it all remains unsolved,
Like has God seeded this one small globe with intelligent beings,
Is earth the only green oasis in a universe of fire
And dead rock, and is God?
Is he? and if not is it worthwhile
Struggling to turn our course around
From cruelty, destruction and war?
I am not alone, except that every I is alone,
Millions of us, sparks of existence, each
Caged in our flesh, driftwood in a cataract
And only the falls ahead
Which reminds me
Today I must wash my hair.
Near as we are to Hell, we are near to Heaven,
And I would be clean.

OLD HABITS

I am not sure, now, that I am not unhappy.
Old habits die hard, the habits of loss
And loneliness are those dark robes
I take from the nail each morning,
                    forgetting
The bright garments of joy that I
                    might wear
Wrapped close around me, sailing out
                    behind
Like the great wings of the wild bird
                    alighting
In sun, on sparkling water.

ONCE

He said to us then
What will you choose?
Something risky, a crash course,
Poverty, disablement?

There are many troubled times.
We could fit you in
Wars, plague, drought

Or would you rather
Take things slowly,
The silver spoon?

There are many mansions,
But these may be booby-trapped.

Down there, you will forget all this.
All evidence is removed.
Undoubtedly they will tell you
God is dead,
And you will believe it.

EMPTYING THE BIN

How good I feel when
Noticing the bin is full
I haul the black sack up by its ears
And knot them. Our rubbish
Must not disfigure the lane
As it waits for its consumption
By the iron-toothed lorry.

Outside I set it
Alongside those shameless others
Gaping, disgorging
The detritus of their nights and days.

Back in the house I feel crowned.
Nothing else that I do this day
Will over-top that one useful well-done thing.
No other success will match it,
No blunder, forgetful, scratch it,
No slovenly hour can touch it.
Whatever befalls, I can say
Today I emptied the bin.

ON A FINE DAY

On that day the sun
Was a giant rose in the sky
Pouring down beauty in falls of light
And the trees, thick leaved, held their heads
Like blossom, massive green roses
Curbing the field which spread its turf
Forever under the sky, with clouds sailing
Thoughtful ships of flowers, white roses, some
Unshipped and floating singly, idly in the blue;
And he, at the largest and most precious flower,
Rose of noble descent, his devotion
As he bent to its face ennobling him
While she, housemaid to a clematis,
Hair-dressing the bushes, neat
And slender as a lily
Harvested the weather, gold in her hands.

REFLECTIONS

A woodland path
After weeks of rain.
A pool had gathered there
And trapped another sky
Behind a treetop trellis.

I gazed down at up, the infinite underfoot.

At the opposite end a little dog
About to drink desisted, surprised
To see a little dog about to drink,
And they stood a moment
Chin to chin.

QUIET

I went outside.
The air was keen, and quiet,
Like a good friend.

The empty milk bottles
Dropped quietly into place.

I went, in soft shoes,
To see if the bulbs were showing;
I saw young ivy leaves, growing.

Beside me, I heard a quiet snap
And, looking, saw through the hedge
A horse, just a shadow.

I moved, quietly, nearer, to see him,
Perhaps exchange a word,

But he leapt, and bolted
In one large brown caper
Across the field.

'Sorry,' I said.

Indoors, I wanted to say
'I frightened the horse'
And so on.

But in his armchair
He was quiet,
The radio sprinkling
The air with sweet music,
His hand, holding his book to the light,
Illuminated.

Saying nothing,
In soft shoes,
I crossed the room.

THE NOISE WITHIN

The door closes on the last wave
As the last one leaves.
Inside, the clock ticks again,
The refrigerator trills
And a tap lets fall a tear
Which plucks a note from water in a pan.
Chairs creak as they re-shape.

She stands still, unused to the absence
Of demand, or duty, or concern,
And all the noise.

A DEAD BLUE-TIT

We picked up the tiny un-moving thing
Which had been a bird so quick on the wing,
So alert on a branch that no eye could catch
What now we studied, laid stitch along stitch,
Feather by feather, of soft-coloured thread,
Its body embroidered in contrast and shade,
And open, smoke-coloured, transparent, the wing
Glass, like the window at which it had flown
As if into air, and by that was brought down.

OWL-DROP

They were tall as they stood there,
Or I felt they were; they talked
Above my head, of engines, gears and fuel-pipes,
And the two big wars.

My thoughts, I suppose,
Should have been of saucepans and soap-powder,
But weren't.

I watched the after-glow
Seeping upwards from the bleached grasses.
Just unexceptional ground, but so beautiful.

And the peach-skin of the sky
And the faint star, a pleasure
One could not wish to be brighter.

I panned around
To a tall thin tree, leaf-mantled;
And just in time, for a black shape
Evolved in silence from the leaves

And dropped so fast
I almost lost it.

They had gone on
To Hurricanes and Spitfires.
My bomber was neat
And innocent.

AFTERNOON IN SEPTEMBER

How wonderful, how rare it is
To sit out under the sky which seems
One great face that gazes
With infinite interest. We
In our little wooden chairs amongst the grass
Are hardly more to that above
Than the flat-winged butterflies that
Flutter here or there then settle
Like black pansies where they will.

Look up at that soft seethe of grey,
Its roving thoughts. See an island floating
Miles above yet close,
Intimate as if its eyes
Opened on us, its mouth of mist
Murmured a language that once we knew.

A sudden rush of wings across,
Low spurt of light spiked from the west,
The distances above us
And the multitudes under our feet,
All are native where we are exiles
Trying to return, trying
To recover the forgotten tongue.

SUMMER AND EVENING

Summer, and evening, and black dogs leap
In mild, silent grace across
The western heliotrope, a cyclamen flush
Still lingering low down. The glasses
Register change and, tapped, flick back
To stormy. Sense of loss, the fine
Heat of the weather gone, the roses
Sunsetting on black lawns, and a late bird
Ringing an empty wine-glass. Come
Soon back, my love, I fear the dogs
Will ravage all the sky and leave
No light for us to find each other by.

THE COMET

Someone asked us if we'd seen the comet,
Rapped on our door to tell us it was there,
And we rushed outside.

Below the bank and the ragged hedge
I stood in the lane and gazed, naked-eyed
Into the nameless dark, where something moved.

'It's gone again,' they said ' - just a glimpse,
But there's a mist shifting - there, I saw it then.'
But my eyes showed me nothing but`a feeling.

I had a soft quiet rush of a sensation,
A comet-feeling, a feather-broom, squirrel-tail effect
Of an intense slow-speed journeying up there

Where I buried my face and eyes into the dark
As if it was fur, and I could see a pulse, a drift
Swell and shake, disturbed by something passing.

'Shall we go in?' someone said. 'We've seen
What there is to see.'

LATE SWINGS

A swing is never empty.
Even when the child is gone
Into sleep or further,
And you catch it still, be sure
It has only just died down
From riotous arcs.

When we entered the empty green our ghosts
Ran us through the swirling dusk
To the bank of swings. We gave ourselves
To the easy flying, swallows
On evening sweeps, while far away
The lights of cars through trees
Swung out and burned.

'Close your eyes,' said my husband.
I did, and swam
Like a swan in the green, soft dark.

FINDING THE CURVE

The poem touched me, and it sprang
Into the curve as a rainbow does
When sunbeams leap through the drenched air.

It has no reality yet, its life
No cogency, its purpose
Hidden in that place where rainbows are
Before they come. I am to hold it,
Keep it in balance, tense, as a bow
Holds the arrow before it flies.

So it is a matter of fingers and the pen
And my heart which have the knowledge
Which I, earthbound, must find and trust
Then let the arrow go,
Watch the rainbow curve as it becomes
A leaping horse, or the seagulls I saw
Like flying stars on a black sky.